PARTICIPANT WORKBOOK

REALITY-BASED LEADERSHIP
Workshop

CY WAKEMAN

WILEY

Cover image: Thinkstock

Cover design: Adrian Morgan

For additional copies/bulk purchases of this book in the U.S. please contact 800-274-4434.

For additional copies or bulk purchases of this book or to learn more about Wiley's Workplace Learning offerings, please contact us toll free at 1-866-888-5159 or by email at workplacelearning@wiley.com.

Wiley also publishes its books in a variety of electronic formats and by print-on-demand. Some material included with standard print versions of this book may not be included in e-books or in print-on-demand. If the version of this book that you purchased references media such as a CD or DVD that was not included in your purchase, you may download this material at http://booksupport.wiley.com. For more information about Wiley products, visit www.wiley.com.

ISBN: 978-1-118-540442

Printed in the United States of America

Printing 10 9 8 7 6 5 4 3 2 1

Contents

Welcome!

I am confident that you will begin leading differently immediately following this workshop. To help with that, after each section in this workbook I have offered a bottom-line idea that I hope you adopt immediately.

At Cy Wakeman, Inc., we are happy to help you as you travel along your leadership journey. All we ask is that you, too, ditch the drama and help yourself and others turn excuses into results.

Welcome to Reality-Based Leadership!

Fondly,

Cy Wakeman

Founder and CEO, Cy Wakeman, Inc.

Save the drama for your momma.

Unknown

Workshop Outcomes

Our hopes for you are simple—that you will change the way you think about your circumstances, and the circumstances of the people you lead, so that you ditch the drama, restore sanity to the workplace, and turn excuses into results. You will

- Learn to diffuse drama and lead the person in front of you;

- Increase your awareness of mindsets that will help you to find peace at work by uncovering destructive thought patterns within yourself and others;

- Learn ways to restore sanity to the workplace by empowering others to focus on the facts and think for themselves; and

- Understand new ways to demonstrate Reality-Based Leadership competencies to help you lead your team to results.

The job of a leader is to conserve the
energy about to be consumed in drama and
redirect it toward efforts that have better ROI.

Cy Wakeman

Using This Workbook

We realize it is uncomfortable to share your deepest thoughts out loud. You don't have to, but we definitely would like for you to capture those thoughts by writing them down. They will be good reference notes for you to pull out later as you work to develop your Reality-Based Leadership skills.

At the end of each section, there's a place to capture the answers to two questions:

- What insights did you have?
- What action are you going to take based on those insights?

There are places throughout the workbook titled "The Reality-Based Leader's Bottom Line." These sections epitomize the main point the author wanted you to absorb. In this section you may find simple tools that you can employ immediately. Think about this and document any related thoughts you have or follow-up actions for you to take.

The Basics

Definition of Reality

reality |rēˈalətē|

noun (pl. realities)

1 the world or the state of things as they actually exist, as opposed to an idealistic or notional idea of them.

Why We Are Here

The average person spends two hours per day in drama. When you look at optimizing your resources and redirecting this energy toward focusing on results, the payback could be enormous. Excuses and drama are getting in the way of producing positive business results.

According to a recent Gallup poll, what percentage of employees considers quitting their job daily?

- a. Less than 20 percent
- b. Nearly half
- c. Greater than 50 percent
- d. Other:

If people were actually quitting at the rate that they *think* about quitting, we would be alarmed. Worse, they continue to go to work every day, showing up and collecting paychecks, while completely checked out emotionally. *Leaders sometimes* spend their time working on increasing the engagement of employees by trying to change the circumstances around them. *The truth is that leaders cannot change every circumstance to make people happy.*

Be very clear; each one of us is always co-creating our current and future realities.

Cy Wakeman

Notes

Find Peace at Work

Refuse to Argue with Reality

Arguing about situations that are unlikely to change does not result in improved business results and is therefore wasted effort. It is a fight you are sure to lose, but only 100 percent of the time.

The Reality-Based Leader's Bottom Line

Regardless of the circumstances facing you, ask yourself, "What can I do next to add the most value?"

Edit the Story

> In order to restore peace in your life, you need to understand that the source of your suffering is not what happens to you, but the stories you make up about what happens to you.
>
> *Cy Wakeman*

As you lead, watch for Three Common Stories:

- *Victim Stories:* "It's not my fault." These stories make us out to be innocent sufferers.

- *Villain Stories:* "It's all your fault." These tales emphasize others' nasty qualities.

- *Helpless Stories:* "There's nothing else I can do." These stories convince us that we have no options for taking healthy action.

Edit Stories Exercise

Think of a situation that frustrated you or a direct report recently at work. Describe it here.

Next, write down your or his/her true thoughts, uncensored. What snarky things were you (he/she) thinking? What theory was this event proving to be true? What meaning was being assigning to this event? ("I always. . . ," "They never/always. . . ," "They should/shouldn't. . . ," "It's not right that. . . ," "This means that. . . ."

Next, be clear about what is true. Go back through your original account and underline ONLY the statements that are actually true.

Amazing what we can create from a simple event isn't it?

> ### The Reality-Based Leader's Bottom Line
> When you find yourself upset, ask "What do I know for sure?"

Notes

Reality–Based Leadership

Depersonalize Feedback

Feedback Disparity Exercise

If someone's performance is hindering results, and quite frankly driving you mad, how likely is it that you would share that feedback with the person directly?

Highly Unlikely   Highly Likely

1   2   3   4   5   6   7   8   9   10

Now . . . if your performance is hindering someone else's results and driving him or her mad, how likely is it that you want the person to share the information with you?

Highly Unlikely   Highly Likely

1   2   3   4   5   6   7   8   9   10

Is there is a difference in your answers to the two questions? If so, why is that?

People generally think they would rather receive feedback than give feedback. However, constructive and helpful feedback should flow freely in all directions.

Let's be clear: lack of feedback is the root cause of all employee issues.

Cy Wakeman

Reality–Based Leadership

One-on-One Meeting Agenda

If you have a small team, it is ideal to plan a quick one-on-one with each of your people once a week. The benefit of this is that you keep abreast of any issues as they arise, so they don't become bigger issues, and your people always know when their next scheduled one-on-one is, so they can save up any non-critical questions for the meeting. Here's an example of an agenda for such a meeting:

Name: _____

Week ending: _____

What has been the most challenging part of your week?

What has been the most rewarding part of your week?

Goals or planned actions for the week:

_____

_____

_____

_____

Progress on the goals or planned actions:

Issues to review:

Resources needed:

_____

_____

_____

Questions:

Critical Feedback to Share

1. Here is what you are doing that is helpful:

2. This is what you are doing that is hindering results:

Next week's goals or planned actions:

_____

_____

_____

_____

_____

_____

The Reality-Based Leader's Bottom Line

Share with your employees regularly what they are doing that is helpful and what they are doing that hinders.

For more information on feedback, check out *What Did You Say? The Art of Giving and Receiving Feedback* by Charles Seashore.

Find Peace at Work: Call to Action

Refuse to argue with reality and ask, *"How can I help?*

Edit your story and ask, *"What do I know for sure?"*

Depersonalize feedback and ask others, *"What do I do that's helpful?"* and *"What do I do that hinders?"*

What insights did you have?

What action are you going to take based on those insights?

Restore Sanity to the Workplace

I am often accused of playing favorites. My response?
You bet I play favorites; would you like to be one?

Cy Wakeman

Work with the Willing

What percentage of people in organizations would we typically label as "the willing" or "visionaries"?

Answer: _____

Three Types of Employees

- Resistant
- Maintenance
- Visionaries

Working with the willing is code for "play favorites." In what situations is it okay to play favorites? In what situations should you avoid favoritism?

Redirect your focus to the top 20 percent—the willing. If you focus your energy and attention on those in resistance, you are paying them to critique and sabotage your plan and the other people you lead will notice. They want attention, too, and you'll have shown them exactly how to get it. Before long, many more of your people (who are in maintenance mode) will be slouching low in their chairs, joining the resistance movement. Can you blame them?

The Reality-Based Leader's Bottom Line

Play favorites. Others will likely sign up once they see what gets attention from you. Consider telling your direct reports what it takes to be one of your favorites.

Lead First, Manage Second

Staying on Track

Manager's Role

Leader's Role

Delegating is a tool a leader can use to develop new skills in his or her direct reports.

The Reality-Based Leader's Bottom Line

Stop sympathizing with your employees and instead empathize with them. Then call them to greatness.

Bulletproof Your Employees

Video Notes

> "Whether you believe something is possible or impossible, you will be right."

What does this statement mean to you?

If we aren't bulletproof, our initial reactions to adversity are . . .

Surprise
Panic
Blame

The Reality-Based Leader's Bottom Line

Build confidence in your employees that anything is possible. Why? Because one must think he or she can before he or she actually can. Work on mindsets and the behavior will come.

Call to Action

Work with the Willing and ask, *"Who are my high-value players and how can I leverage them?"*

Lead First, Manage Second and ask *"Am I coaching and developing each person on my team on an individual basis?"*

Bulletproof Your Employees and regularly ask them *"What else did you try?"* and *"What could be good reasons you are in this situation?"*

What insights did you have?

What action are you going to take based on those insights?

Re-Engagement

Lead Your Team to Results

Achieving Results in Changing Times

If you want to protect your organization from learned helplessness and set it up for success, regardless of changing circumstances, you must work on two skills.

> Skill 1: The ability to _____ appropriately to adversity
>
> Skill 2: A profound commitment to succeed in _____ of the facts.

Our first reactions to change are rarely helpful. What are some initial responses you personally have when faced with change?

Learned Helplessness

When a person has learned to behave helplessly to avoid perceived unpleasant results, failing to respond even though opportunities exist to improve the situation. Usually occurs when there have been several failed attempts in the past.

How might having a defense help you be prepared to offset your initial responses if they are counterproductive?

How might you help those you lead to redirect their focus when they have counterproductive reactions to change?

Negative Brainstorming Exercise

Instructions:

1. Considering a given directive or issue, each individual introduces his or her concerns, one at a time, in front of the group, while a recorder writes them on a flip chart or whiteboard (leaving ample space between entries). The other members of the group must refrain from discussion, critique, or disagreement and wait their turns. The process continues until the group has exhausted its list of concerns and all are documented.

2. Next, taking it risk by risk, determine the probability of each risk actually manifesting itself. Assign each a probability of High, Medium, or Low.

3. Again, taking it risk by risk, determine the potential impact of each risk. Assign each an impact rating of High, Medium, or Low.

4. Now, create strategies to mitigate each risk. The team will make a determination about where to best apply its energy and resources based on the combination of probability and impact for each risk.

A sample format for this activity is provided on the next page.

Negative Brainstorming Grid

Risks	Probability	Impact	Action
	High Med Low	High Med Low	
From: Why we can't. . .			To: How we can. . .

The Reality-Based Leader's Bottom Line

Individuals may identify problems but cross-functional teamwork may be necessary to solve problems. Do not buy into the limiting belief that people should only come to you with solutions. This idea was likely born out of a need to stop people from whining and complaining. Wouldn't it be more direct to simply tell them that their whining is hindering the team's efforts? Try negative brainstorming to get things done.

Stop Judging

Outlaw the option of judging a team member. Force yourself and those you work with to ask *"How can I help?"*

Great leaders insist that all team members stop judging and start helping.

Cy Wakeman

The Reality-Based Leader's Bottom Line

The moment you start judging and you tell anyone besides your spouse, partner, or pet, you forfeit the higher ground and are no longer helping.

Value Action Over Opinion

What percentage of employees in an organization are *actually* decision-makers?

a. 10%

b. 25%

c. 50%

d. Other ____

If you are a decision-maker, you may wish to consult with people who have relevant expertise and experience. The opinions of people with no relevant expertise are of little value to you. So avoid gathering opinions for the sake of inclusiveness. Does this mean that you don't care about these people as valuable members of the team? Absolutely not! It's actually one of several good reasons not to encourage them to editorialize about decisions, and instead make it clear to them that their action—in executing the plan, mitigating its risks, and making it work for your customers—is far more valuable to the company.

The Reality-Based Leader's Bottom Line

Execution is what matters most, not effort.

Organizational Alignment

As a leader, you have to keep your personal opinions related to directives passed down to you just that—personal. Do not share how you feel about a directive with your direct reports. Criticizing any decision made by another level of your leadership team is a cardinal sin. If your team members can recognize that you are not supportive of a decision, even though you're heading the implementation plans, you have failed them in one of the worst possible ways.

Just say "yes," then figure out how to make it happen. If you are asked for feedback about a plan, know that the decision-maker is asking for your expertise—not editorials.

The Reality-Based Leader's Bottom Line

The Internet has basically replaced you as a provider of information. Keep your opinion to yourself unless you are being helpful to the organization; get quickly on to saying "yes" and to "winning."

Driving for Results

Don't lower the bar whatever you do. Effort does not equate to winning. Winning is equated to winning.

There are two distinct camps in the business world today: leaders whose teams have failed to measure up, who work diligently to deliver the "facts" in the form of reasons, stories, and excuses; and leaders whose teams have delivered results in spite of the same "facts." The difference between these two camps lies not in their circumstances, but the path that the leaders chose to take. Check out the Results Circle for a graphic illustration of the consequences of each approach.

Results Circle

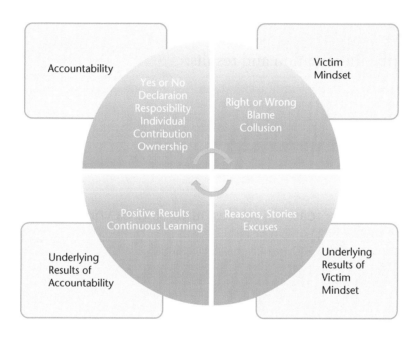

Accountability

Yes or No
Declaraion
Resposibility
Individual
Contribution
Ownership

Victim
Mindset

Right or Wrong
Blame
Collusion

Positive Results
Continuous Learning

Reasons, Stories
Excuses

Underlying
Results of
Accountability

Underlying
Results of
Victim
Mindset

If it is to be, it is up to me.

William H. Johnson

Personal Example of Less-Than-Ideal Results

Briefly describe the situation and results:

What are some of the reasons, stories, and excuses you have about that issue?

Notes from Coaching Session

- What have you tried to overcome those stories?
- What else have you tried?

Questions to Ask When Accounting for Results

■ What were your results? Did you succeed or not? (Watch out for the individual or team lowering the standard, wanting to believe that he or she "did pretty well considering the circumstances," as if a person should receive extra points for challenges.)

■ What happened? (Listen for their stories. Are they closely accounting for the facts and their behavior?)

■ How do you account for your results? (Listen for "I," not "we," or "they" or "you.")

■ What did you believe?

- How did that belief affect your behavior, attitude, creativity, and choices?

- What were the facts? What did you know or what do we know for sure?

- How committed were you? How bought-in were you?

- What could you change to ensure your success in the future? (Listen to make sure that changes are in the first person, and not about having more resources, changing others, or changing their reality and circumstances.)

- What are you committing to in the future? (Have people write it down—that is their new development plan—and then hold them to it.)

The Reality-Based Leader's Bottom Line

Unfavorable circumstances are not the reasons why you can't succeed, they are the reasons you MUST succeed.

Call to Action

Stop judging and ask, *"How can I help?"*

Align with the organization by asking "What can I do" to gain agreement with the decisions that have been made.

Drive for results by focusing on your goals and by demonstrating ownership and keeping those goals in front of your team.

What insights did you have?

What action are you going to take based on those insights?

Development Plan

Name: _____ Start Date: _____

Current role: _____

Key themes from the Reality-Based Leadership Self-Assessment:

_____

_____

_____

_____

Objectives and Action Steps

Objective 1: _____

Action Step: _____

Action Step: _____

Completion Date: _____

Sponsor: _____

Objective 2: _____

Action Step: _____

Action Step: _____

Completion Date: _____

Sponsor: _____

Signature: _____

Manager's Signature: _____

Close

In this session, you've been given some unconventional wisdom about how to strengthen your working relationships, create bullet-proof teams, and return peace, sanity, and results to your workplace. Think about this: You spend more time with your co-workers than you do with almost anyone else. It's essential that you find a way not only to be "real" with these people, but also to make the most of what can end up being some of the best years of your life. It's up to you whether your workday is an ordeal in the company of Jerks and Idiots or a time when camaraderie and succeeding in spite of your circumstances brings you satisfaction and profit.

The great thing about life is that every day we have a new shot at it. If your office atmosphere leaves a lot to be desired, it's in your power to begin creating a better place to work, starting now, with the principles you've learned in this session.

The Reality-Based Leader's Manifesto

We, as Reality-Based Leaders. . .

- Refuse to argue with reality

- Are very careful about what we think we know for sure

- Lead first, manage second

- Greet change with a simple "good to know"

- Depersonalize feedback—whatever the source

- Ask ourselves, "What is the next right thing I can do to add the most value?"

- Ask others, "How can I help?" instead of judging and blaming

- Work to find the opportunity in every challenge

- Work harder at being happy than at being right

- Work with the willing

- Value action over opinion

It's one thing to grasp these principles intellectually and another to apply them, and ultimately make them part of your organization's DNA. To support your efforts, check out www.realitybasedleadership.com, where you will gain privileged access to a world of coaching resources and extra content to help you become a Reality-Based Leader, including:

- A message board where you can post questions

- Access to weekly podcasts, live and archived

- A call-in number to participate in group coaching calls

- Access to extra assessments and tests

- Reality-Based Leadership blog

- Audio and video recordings of seminars and sessions

Additional Resources

These additional books, articles, and websites related to the content in the *Reality-Based Leadership Workshop* will provide you additional perspective and insight as you work to become a reality-based leader.

Books and Articles

For Yourself

Feeling good matters in the workplace. (2013). *Gallup Management Journal*. Available: http://businessjournal.gallup.com/content/20770/Gallup-Study-Feeling-Good-Matters-Workplace.aspx.

Feldman, C. (2005). *Heart of wisdom, mind of calm: Guided meditations to deepen your spiritual practice*. London: Element.

Heffner, C.L. (2011, November 29). Learned helplessness in personality synopsis at ALLPSYCH Online. Personality Synopsis. Available: http://allpsych.com/personalitysynopsis/learned_helplessness.html.

Kuhn, H.W., Nirenberg, L., Sarnak, P., & Weisfield, M. (1995). *Duke Mathematical Journal*, 81.

Seligman, M. (2008, July). The new era of positive psychology (video). Available: www.ted.com/talks/martin_seligman_on_the_state_of_psychology.html (TED: Ideas Worth Spreading)

Reh, F.J. (2013, January 15). Pareto's principle: The 80-20 rule. Available: http://management.about.com/cs/generalmanagement/a/Pareto081202.htm (About.com Management)

Rock, D. (2007). *Quiet leadership: Six steps to transforming performance at work: Help people think better—Don't tell them what to do!* (pp. 1–27). New York: HarperCollins.

Seashore, C.N., Seashore, E.W., & Weinberg, G.M. (1997). *What did you say? The art of giving and receiving feedback*. Columbia, MD: Bingham House.

Wakeman, C. (2010). *Reality-based leadership: Ditch the drama, restore sanity to the workplace, and turn excuses into results*. San Francisco: Jossey-Bass.

Weber, L. (2013, March 27). Bad at their jobs and loving it (web blog post). *Wall Street Journal*. Available: http://blogs.wsj.com/atwork/2013/03/27/bad-at-their-jobs-and-loving-it/

For Your Direct Reports

Wakeman, C. (2013). *Reality-based rules of the workplace: Know what boosts your value, kills your chances, and will make you happier*. San Francisco: Jossey-Bass. This book brings Cy's powerful message about ditching the drama and becoming a reality-based thinker directly to the employee.

Website

At www.bulletprooftalent.com, learn more about Cy Wakeman's approach to engagement surveys and read whitepapers that support adding a level of questioning to traditional engagement surveys.

About the Author

Cy Wakeman is a dynamic keynote speaker advocating a revolutionary new approach to leadership. Her groundbreaking ideas are featured in *The Wall Street Journal, The New York Times, The New York Post*, and SHRM.com. She is a significant thought leader with entertaining podcasts and is a favorite expert blogger on FastCompany.com and Forbes.com. Cy was honored this year in Mumbai, India, where she was awarded the prestigious World HRD Congress Outstanding Leadership Award for her achievements as a global thought leader in 2012. Past recipients of the award include Marshall Goldsmith and David Ulrich. Her book, *Reality Based Leadership: Ditch the Drama, Restore Sanity to the Workplace, and Turn Excuses into Results* (Jossey-Bass, 2010) is now available at all major book retailers and is receiving rave reviews.

Notes

Notes

Notes

Notes

Notes

Notes

Notes

Notes

Notes

Printed and bound by CPI Group (UK) Ltd, Croydon, CR0 4YY

16/04/2025

14658527-0001